HOW TO POUND SOME SENSE INTO A RELIGIOUS NUT JOB

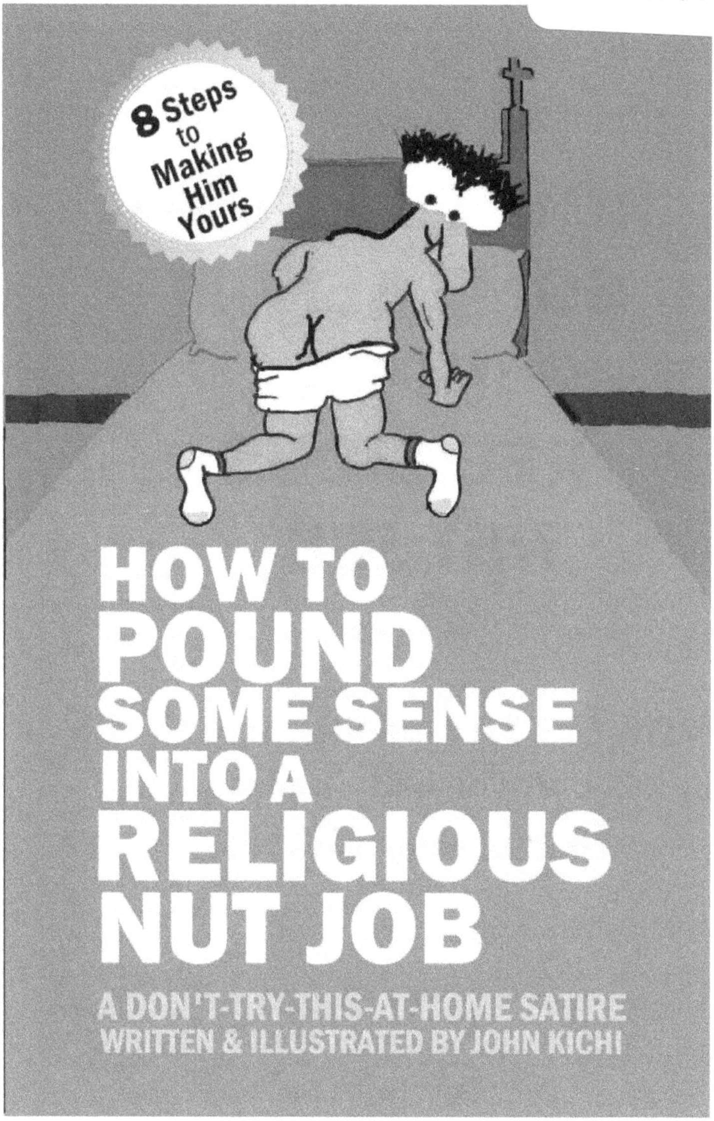

A DON'T-TRY-THIS-AT-HOME SATIRE
WRITTEN & ILLUSTRATED BY JOHN KICHI

"HOW TO POUND SOME SENSE INTO A RELIGIOUS NUT JOB"

A PYGA MEDIA PAPERBACK BOOK
in collaboration with Amazon.com

This book is satire!

DO NOT TRY THIS AT HOME

DATING ANYONE THESE DAYS, ESPECIALLY A MAN WHO THINKS HE'S STRAIGHT, CAN BE PHYSICALLY AND LEGALLY DANGEROUS

Dedicated to
happy
"sodomites"
everywhere

"*The closet-case is always the one in the room*

making the most noise about being straight!"

- *Anonymous*

Author's Preface

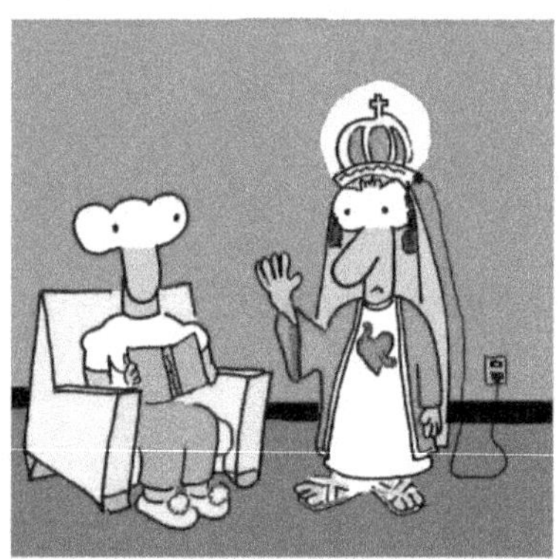

I'm not a religious person. Nor am I convinced an anthropomorphic God exists. But I'm NOT anti-God, I'm not even anti-religion.

What I am "anti" is anyone using God or religion for purposes other than helping them get through their miserable lives in an aloof and dangerous universe. Whatever it takes to get through life, I say. As long as you don't proselytize and sell me your snake oil.

Specifically, I am against the use of God and religion to consolidate power, and self-aggrandize, in a country or a demographic, by scapegoating Gays, Blacks, Latinos, Women and other religions including atheists.

It seems clear to me that no religion has cornered the market on understanding whatever God may or may not exist. No one has a believable explanation for why a God would permit the holocaust, death of infants and suffering in old age. And therefore, no religion should proselytize or market their brand of believing to anyone else.

But Evangelical Christianity is all about marketing and creating a monopoly through hate.

Evangelicals are the unsheathed penis of religion. They want to ejaculate their dogma into weak minds to help grow their brand. They MUST be stopped. We must be the SPERMICIDE.

And the best way to accomplish that is to slow their growth by reducing the volume of their "seed" … or in the vernacular: stop them from reproducing by introducing their young male recruits to the joy of Gay sex.

Introduction

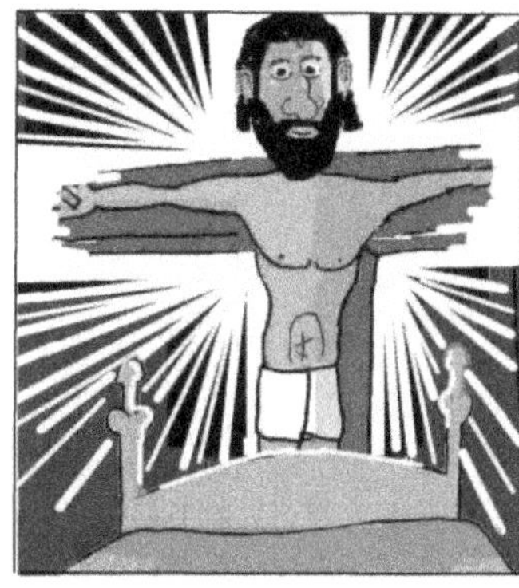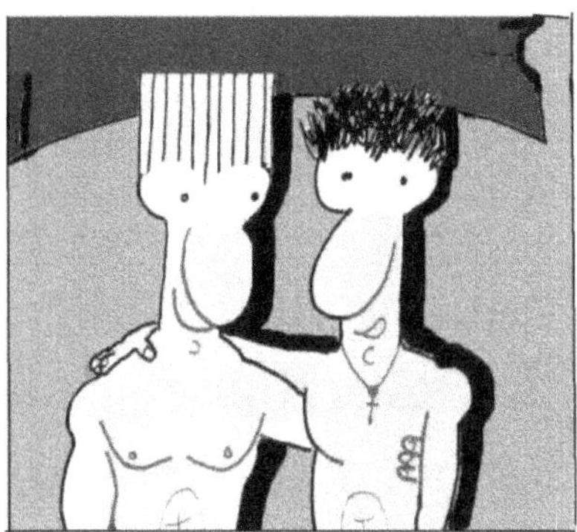

If you've ever been to an Evangelical Christian church service, or heard their spokespeople talk, you know they HATE Gays, Blacks Asians, Mexicans and believe that women should be in the kitchen, barefoot and pregnant. Essentially, they HATE everyone but themselves. It's not a religion based on the teachings of Jesus, it's a tribe.

The experience is frightening. It's not a religion. It's a PAC (Political Action Committee)

So, you may be asking yourself, why then does anyone want to date an Evangelical Christian, even a young Evangelical man with a sculpted chest, bulging biceps and a hot butt?

I'll tell you. Because youth are the source of growth for everything. countries. businesses. ideas. dogma. hate movements. Change the minds of the youth and Evangelical Christianity is dead.

Then you ask, "aren't young Evangelical men stupid shits to believe in their 'sick religion'." The answer is, some are, but not all of them. They are neither stupid or evil. They are deluded and too young to know they have been brainwashed into the service of evil. Many are cowed by their parents who pay their bills and convinced to go along also by peer pressure.

But remember this: religion has little power against raging hormones of young males.

Young evangelicals are the largest group of sexually repressed men in the country. But their church dogma strains against the need these men have for sexual release. Like a balloon inflated to its bursting point, one prick and … bang! You are, so to speak, **that** prick!

The young Evangelical man is a prisoner of his circumstance. He's kept by his family and spoon fed their hate. He is without form of his own and doesn't yet know what he doesn't know.

We're – YOU'RE - going to teach him what he doesn't know which includes the fact that Gay sex is FUN, and that God doesn't care who you love just that you LOVE! Find him and teach him LOVE.

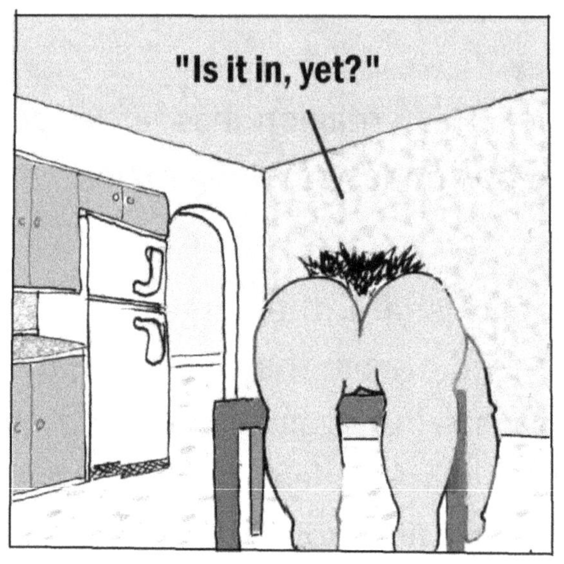

The Eight Step Program

1. FINDING HIM
2. EVALUATING HIM
3. MEETING HIM
4. KNOWING HIM
5. COURTING HIM
6. TEACHING HIM
7. SELLING HIM
8. CLOSING HIM

Step 1

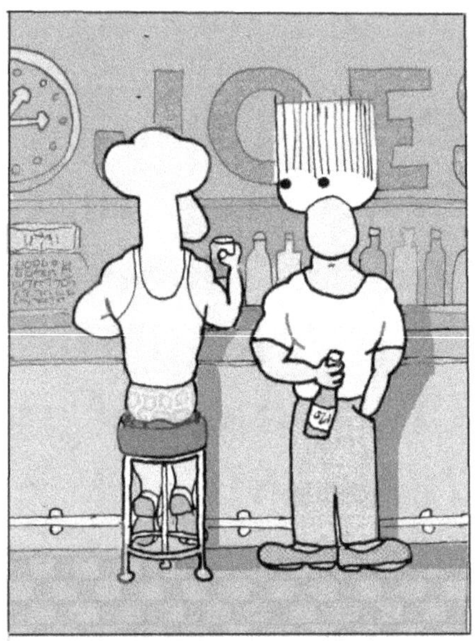

FINDING HIM

The first question you need to answer is where to locate your young male Evangelical target.

You'll need a venue that can be revisited. A venue where men talk to each other freely. And a venue that speaks to the young man's suitability to being deprogrammed (i.e., a venue that demonstrates he has a secular and social side). A church comes to mind, at once. Also, Bible study groups, faith-based charities that need volunteers, and social venues/events at Christian-affiliated universities. But with these venues, you'll need to watch closely for evidence of a secular side.

You may need to temporarily violate many of your own principles just to enter an Evangelical church or university and you WILL stand out unless you work hard to avoid detection. Remember a congregation or a student-body is a closed tribe. And a church is where your target will be self-conscious and on his best behavior. They can smell "the other."

But by being seen at his church you will develop bona fides that your potential convert may appreciate. Be careful that you not over-develop these religious bona fides, as in the end, he could see you as hypocrite and reject you on the grounds that you are blatantly unscrupulous.

Christian-affiliated universities hold a lot of promise especially at the gym. Even religious young men take care of their bodies. It's about looking good for the opposite (or same) sex.

A gym, even a secular, commercial gym, is an excellent venue for detecting and separating the available Evangelical from the rest. It's where men make repeat visits. There's a casual atmosphere. Men routinely engage in conversations without the social stigma attached to male to male bonding in other locations.

Whatever your venue, one factor above all others is important: it must be a setting where you can observe, over time, who might be your best target.

One last thing. Forget bars. A straight bar often springs to mind as a venue almost immediately for many for meeting men and should just as quickly be rejected. Booze, the need for men to be guarded in such places and your serious purpose do not mix.

Step 2

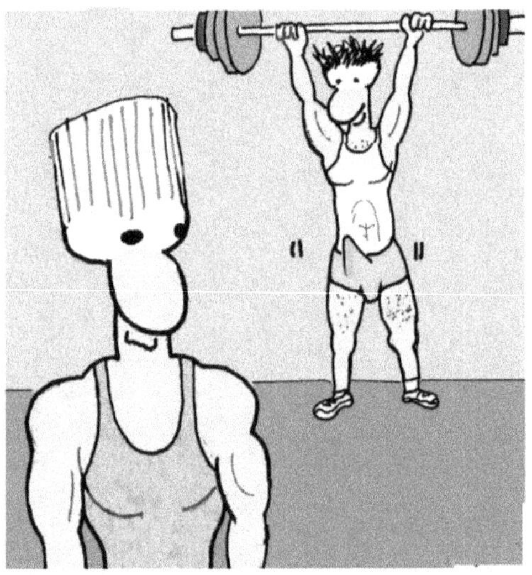

EVALUATING HIM

Wherever you choose to meet your deluded, Evangelical young man you'll need to be selective. You do not want to waste your time on a man who is not a good prospect. You want a man who exhibits signs that he is an Evangelical Christian but potentially susceptible to new ideas and your wiles…. that he is, therefore, a good candidate for persuasion. You don't want to waste time on young Evangelicals hardened by their bad DNA or damaged upbringings. And young men below the age of consent are to be rejected at all cost; besides being jail-bait these young men with hair trigger erections haven't sufficiently developed the number of neurons to process any information other than puberty.

You're looking for young men who are bright enough to receive a new message and can also be bright, attractive ambassadors for our side in the future. Here's what to consider as you evaluate potential candidates.

Over and above that you think he's HOT TAMALES, there's one essential thing to look for when seeking the best prospect: a sign from God. The God of love, that is. During the evaluation phase, you'll inevitably make eye contact with your target. It will be fleeting. Momentary.

Ephemeral. If his eyes linger on yours, even for a millisecond, he could be the one. And if smiles at the same time, you may have struck pay-dirt.

But is he the one? More research is required. Most young Evangelical men travel in packs of like-minded other men to:

> A) avoid men who are not members
>   of their tribe
>   &
> B) avoid the off-chance they will be
>   approached by Gay men
.

This is usually a sub-conscious thing, but it is real and for them, it is visceral. The members of the pack are not aware of the deeply repressed purpose of the pack, but they know it makes them feel safe. Pack animals can be a suitable target, but it will take time to sort through the conversations you overhear and sort through the body language to determine who might be suitable for your purposes.

For a more expeditious result, do consider the young man who travels with a single male companion. This demonstrates an ability to bond, and a degree of socialization above and beyond the pack animal.

It may even hint at one or both men privately, secretly exploring their repressed homosexual feelings for the other. More often than not, your primary target will be the more attractive of the two young men. But either one is fair game.

The young man who consistently is out and about alone may be enticing, and indeed he may also be an Evangelical, but he is alone for a reason. Just make sure the reason is that no one likes him. And if no one likes him, how could he ever be a salesman for OUR tribe?

Without becoming a social butterfly and making a spectacle of yourself, befriend as many men as possible. And try to overhear conversations across the room. "Float like a butterfly, sting like a bee!" as Mohammed Ali said about his boxing-ring strategy. Listen for clues about his likes, dislikes. Where he goes to have fun. What he does if a friend makes an inappropriate joke. He's going to talk as if he has a girlfriend. Yeah, right! He sure won't have a girlfriend for long!

Now, how to rank your possible prospects. You're most likely to have success with:

1.	Men who are neat but not fanatic about their appearance. Grooming shows a degree of self-awareness and self-respect. Over-grooming shows adherence to societal

2.	norms and this man is unlikely to be receptive to new ideas;

3.	Men who do not worship themselves in the mirror. A man who is into himself is impossible to teach because you can't get his attention;

4.   Men who are polite and courteous. A guy that is over-bearing or bullying is a lost cause.

Above all else in making your choice is this: select the man who seems like a person you'd like to be with if he weren't a religious not job; he won't be a religious nut job after you get through with him. Trust your instincts but be careful. Dating – and that's the path you're embarking upon- is always a crap-shoot and changing hearts and minds an even bigger gamble. Just be ready for anything. And be honest with yourself. Admit when you've made a mistake. Oh, you ARE going to make mistakes. Admit it and move on. You're going to need patience with your candidate and yourself.

Step 3

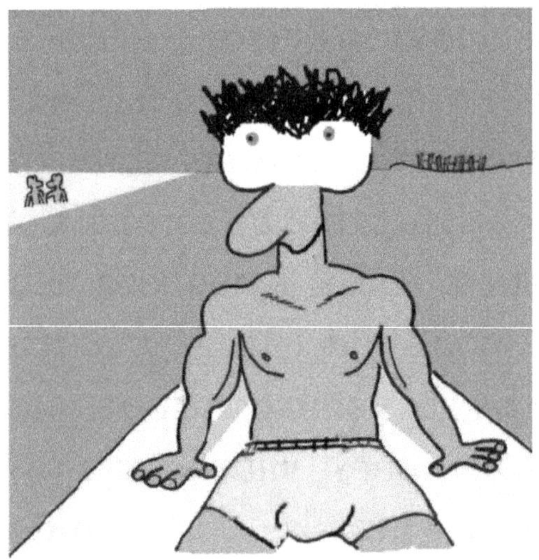

MEETING HIM

After days (and perhaps weeks) of evaluation, you'll have made a selection and want to make contact. This is best done when your young Evangelical is alone. While he is a pack animal, even if only a pack-of-two animal, there will be times, for whatever reason, he WILL be alone.

No doubt, you have your own best way to meet prospective dates. And no doubt, you vary your approach slightly, or even significantly, each time you approach a man. You've learned from experience. All men are different (except for their obsession over sex). One size does not fit all. But it is important you don't learn too much from experience. Because there are very few rules about dating that apply across the board and over time.

The thing to consider when approaching your young evangelical, the thing to keep uppermost in mind, is your goal to be his lover AND teacher. This will stop him from procreating and ruining many lives. So, you'll need to earn his respect from the get-go. And his admiration. His trust. While that is nearly impossible to do on a first encounter, you want to do nothing that limits your chances of earning his esteem eventually. So, tread lightly here. No craziness, no over-the-top humor. No stupid opening lines.

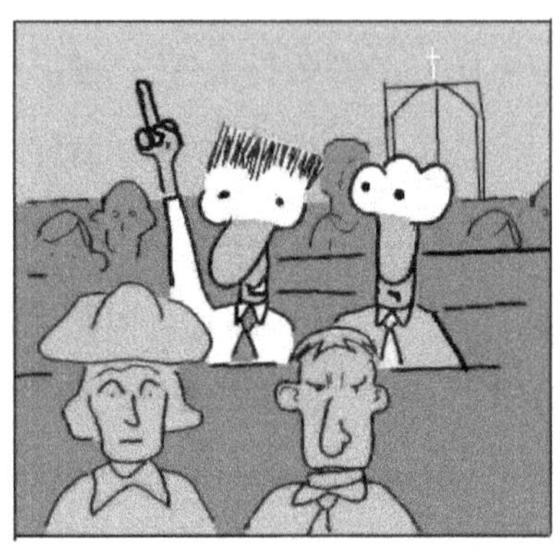

At church, you can let your target see you roll your eyes at any part of the sermon that sounds too much like hell-fire and brimstone, which is probably most of the sermon. He'll likely respond with a smile because deep down he doesn't believe most of that shit and only attends church to please his parents. Remember, **hormones are more powerful than religion.** Later when you see him in the vestibule, you can pretend to apologize for being "sacrilegious." Then, before his family/friends collect him for the ride home, tell him you "owe him one" – perhaps a beer – and get his phone number.

At the gym, I'd recommend offering him a spot on the bench press. If he refuses, tell him why its best to have a spot (go to failure on the last rep) and then tell him he can ask anytime. If he does not ask you for a spot within the next few times you see him, try the more direct approach. Ask him how his workout is going. Discuss nutrition. Then invite him out for a protein shake. If all else fails, tell him you have tickets (buy them) to a sporting event and invite him. If he doesn't respond, let him go. And start looking for someone else.

Out and about in town, in a coffee shop or religious book store or on the street, your job is more difficult. You haven't had the time or opportunity to effectively perform STEP 2 "EVALUATING HIM." So, this is a real crap shoot. you'll have to be quick. And memorable. I recommend the straightforward approach. Walk up to the young man and ask him if he is religious. He'll proudly say yes. Tell him you thought he might be. There's a glow about him.

Explain you'd like to learn more about God (that's not too hypocritical; you DO want to learn more about how his "God" restricts him). Ask if he knows of a Bible group. If he says no, tell him you're heard of one and ask him (after admitting what you're about ask is a bit presumptuous) if he wants to go. Hopefully, he'll say yes, or he'll think about it. Exchange contact information. Done! Except, you'd better find a Bible group in a hurry.

Step 4

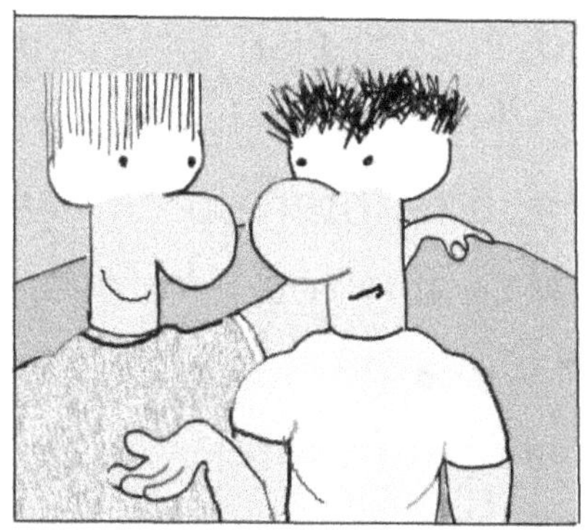

KNOWING HIM

Before you can teach him and/or love him, you need to know him. Or better said, you need to help him know himself. Remember, he's young and has been brainwashed.

We're not going after a one-night stand here. We're trying to create a lasting relationship that will permit the exchange of information ... and, okay, bodily fluids.... but I digress.

Now that you've connected, you'll need to sustain that connection and make it last long enough for you to accomplish your mission(s). You'll never get to know this man if you don't make him believe you're interested in who he is. Listen to him. Make him feel important, even dominant. Let him win arguments that you know you can successfully rebut later. Look him in the eye at all times when speaking to him. Never be judgmental. Draw out his feelings on whatever you're discussing.

Wherever you go with him during your attempt to win him, never forget HIM. He is the reason for your mission. You are out to make HIS life better. In ALL ways! You'll never do that if he doesn't feel that, indeed, your purpose is his welfare.

Be best friends. Be his best friend ever! There is little sweeter in the world than BFBL (Best Fuck Buddy for Life)!

Step 5

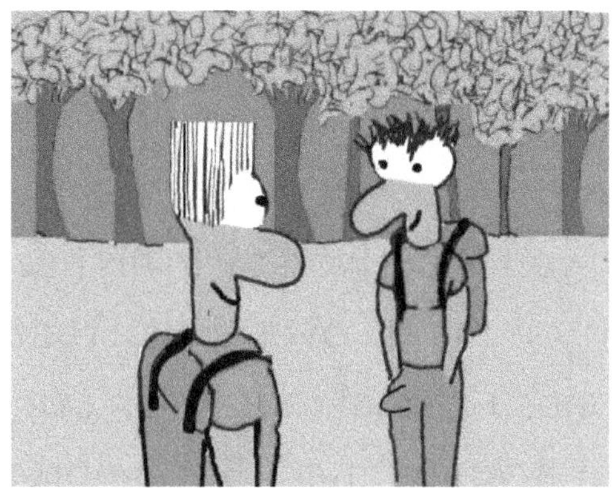

COURTING HIM

Yes, it will be a courtship of a sort. But unlike heterosexual courtship, your goal is not simply getting him between the sheets though many of the same rules apply. You want to win his mind & heart. One key here, is a mix of time spent with friends and time alone with him.

Remember, you're "dating" him but you don't want him to understand that too soon. It's not necessarily duplicitous nor hypocritical because you are trying to help him. Of course, on some subliminal level, he knows what you're doing and, if he continues to date you, on some level he likes it.

And remember, you likely won't win his heart, let along his body or mind, overnight. That may happen. Hormones + sexual repression can be an explosive mix in a young man. But be prepared to be patient. We're talking weeks, even months, not days, of effort.

Courting/dating while not making it seem like that's what you're doing is a challenge. In some ways, it's easier with a man. With a woman, there's always the cultural assumption of the potential for sex. When men bond, it's usually to prevent any underlying attraction from bubbling to the surface. This is why men use sports, sports and more sports - surrogates for the sex act - to tamp down male-on-male sexual imperative. With a male bonding, sex is the subconscious context of the union and sport is the conscious expression. The goal is to prevent the inevitable erection (remember hormones) and maintain the type of closeness that society can accept when two men like each other's company and don't find each other to be ugly.

Now, with your recruit, try to make the dates seem like you're just hanging-out. Masculine activities are paramount but not exclusive. Try to select some venues where you will be alone with him and you can develop a sense of each other and learn to trust each other. For instance, the first time you're alone on an outing with him, make NO advances. Let him trust that you are not simply out for his body.

Hang-out with him as often at his place as yours. Talk about women only if he brings them up. After the initial first date, where the two of you are alone, schedule more private outings where an accidental touch or brushing against each other might happen. But don't go too far with the touching. As incidents of touching happen, pretend they are not happening. Give him the space to understand that he likes them.

Don't buy him presents but do pick-up the entire cost of a meal occasionally. Share your books and DVD collection. Make sure you leave things at his apartment. If you find him leaving things at your apartment "accidentally" this is a sign that your efforts are bearing fruit (no pun intended).

Here's a caveat: don't give in to guilt feelings about being duplicitous. Here's another caveat: if you don't have a few pangs of guilt about what you're doing, you're too callous for a project like this and will not succeed. You're not the right person to commit to helping someone. Remember, you are doing this for his own good. Be brave. Be steadfast. You're also doing this for the betterment of the world.

Step 6

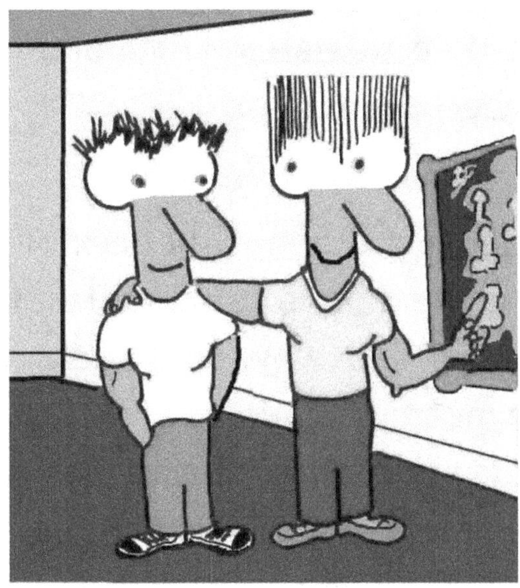

TEACHING HIM

Here's where it gets real. Where you begin to plant doubts about Evangelical dogma. And he'll listen because you've already convinced him, on some deep psychological level, he may not be heterosexual.

You'll need to be as knowledgeable about theology as you are about the male anatomy, i.e. penis. So, it's time to start reading and learn. You're his teacher! His mentor.

He's likely never heard about the lack of trust scholars have with **who** wrote scriptures, **when** they were written and **why**. He's likely never heard that the meaning of words and phrases in the ancient texts are different than similar words used today. He's never learned that ancient texts were translated and translated and mistranslated. And he's for sure never been told that the ancient texts were largely political documents.

You'll be teaching him all that. But remember that you need to be letting him know you're also learning from him. This can't be one-sided. Make sure you often discuss theological issues that you can agree with him on.

To defend your position, you'll want to get updated on the arguments for and against God, for and against religion, for and against evolution, & for and against biblical scriptures condemning homosexuality. To argue a position, you need to know both sides.

Here's a short-list of 8 books I recommend, and I suggest you read them in this order:

1) **<u>A HISTORY OF GOD</u>** by Karen Armstrong
A dispassionate account of the unseemly, violent and often-political history of the world's religions by a former Catholic nun

2) **<u>MISQUOTING JESUS</u>** by Bart Ehrman
Shines a spotlight on the phrases and keywords that Evangelicals use to disavow "the other," showing the Bible to have been mistranslated and miscopied and created for political purposes

3) **<u>THE BIBLE'S "YES" TO SAME-SEX MARRIAGE</u>** by Mark Achtemeier
The title says it all.

4) **<u>THE GOD DELUSION</u>** by Richard Dawkins
A refutation of all things religious by one of the most public and articulate atheists of our time. You'll be blown away by the strength and elegance of Dawkins' arguments and evidence.

5) **<u>THE BLIND WATCHMAKER</u>** by Richard Dawkins
A step by step explanation of the workings of evolution that is a delight to read.

6) **<u>WONDERFUL LIFE</u>** by Stephen J. Gould
A take down of anti-evolution propaganda by a subtle portrayal of the preponderance of evidence supporting evolution

7) **<u>A BRIEF ILLUSTRATED EVOLUTION OF RELIGION</u>** by J.A.Kichi
A sharp, illustrated satire of the psychological history of religion. It's a hoot even If I say so myself.

8) **<u>A LANGUAGE OLDER THAN WORDS</u>** by Eric Jensen
A beautiful, almost poetic, treatise on the wonder of all things living and the connection that exists among species. This book could make you a better person.

Some of you may not be avid readers and a list of "required" reading will be too daunting. Another way to become a credible teacher for your young Evangelical recruit, is to at least understand the major talking points and research information that supports these positions.

You'll want to get across **these important points**:

1)   Gospels written decades after Jesus died and no one knows exactly by who;
2)   Scripture has been mistranslated and misunderstood in the mist of time;
3)   Jesus was a political "messiah" (one of thousands at the time) who came along at the peak of Judea's fight against Rome, or he would have never been remembered;

4)	The sacking of the temple of Jerusalem in 70 A.D. destroyed any physical records of Jesus' 3 years of preaching, and consequently his history is rewritten up to 100 years after his death and mostly for political propaganda;
5)	Religion was and is used to gain political control over the tribes of early man;
6)	Homosexuals were punished and hated by the tribe because a constant harvest of strong young men were needed to protect the tribe and harvest crops.

<>

You probably ought to position yourself with your recruit as neither an atheist, agnostic or religious man but as someone who sees the merits of all sides. You might say something like:

"If there's a God, I don't think any
religion really knows who He is."

... or ...

"In ancient times when the scriptures were written, people with bad eyesight didn't have glasses to correct their vision, the nights were black as pitch without electricity, and the woods were sufficiently scary to make most people superstitious."

But remember you are also responsible for introducing your ward to the broader cultural context that supports a liberal world view, so you'll need to become conversational about many things including government, physics, science, medicine, sociology,

And remember, too, that opinion that ignores fact-based empirical evidence is just bloviating. Offer facts, examples and reference history.

Your new convert is your new boyfriend. Help him to be all the man he can be. He'll thank you for it. Eventually.

Step 7

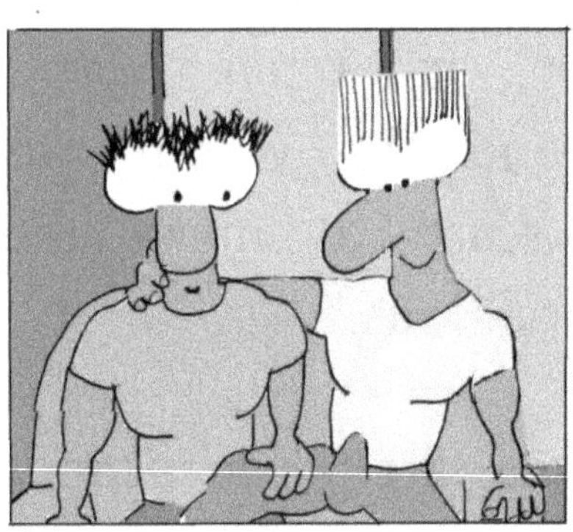

SELLING HIM

By now, you should have a good idea if your young Evangelical has any sales resistance left to fend off you and your ideas. If he did, he'd likely have stopped seeing you a while ago.

Consequently, at this point you probably can feel his acquiesce. So, you're likely developing some confidence. But beware of over confidence.

Nothing is certain, and you should **NOT** approach STEP 7 as if you've already won, but merely that you are **likely** to win, all the while conforming to basic norms of politeness, respect, sexual propriety and tenderness.

Over your courting experience, you have been sitting closer and closer to him. Now is the time to amp that up. In a series of consecutive "dates" you need to narrow the physical gap between you on the couch. And become increasingly, but gradually, more physical.

Slap his leg when a touchdown is made if you're watching football. Put your hand on his shoulder if you want to get his attention. Touch him EVERY TIME you think it's justifiable.

You're setting the stage for the leap across his abyss of self-denial. You're building bridges.

Step 8

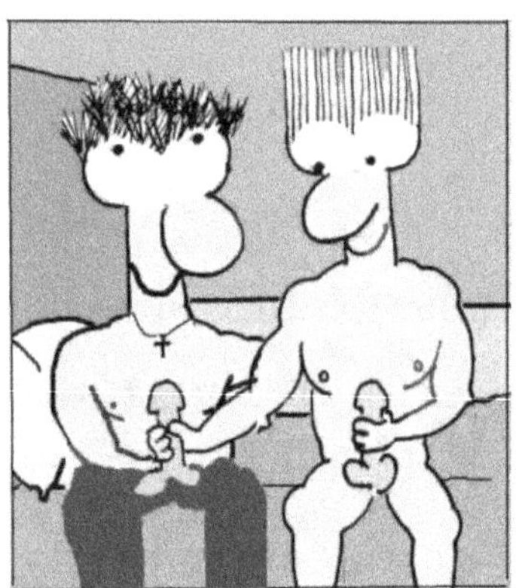

CLOSING HIM

This step could also be called OPENING HIM UP because that's what you want to do to his mind and ... let's face it .... his butthole.

On the night you select as appropriate to make THE pass, don't schedule anything out of the ordinary. If it's his turn to host you, go to his place. If it's your turn, hook up at your apartment. The ostensible reason for hanging out should be an ordinary one. And your physical proximity and chatter should be ordinary, but typical, of the closeness you've developed.

As the big moment draws near, you can tell if he's ready in two ways:

1)   he's permitted your bodies to gently touch and pretend to not notice
&
2)   he continues to maintain eye contact with you

But here's a caveat. Book solutions to human interaction can't possibly take into account every possible turn of events or personality quirk. Even after years of close association, couples – heterosexual and homosexual – complain that they don't really understand each other. Part of that divide is created by the ways people change over time. Even in the short amount of time you've known your young Evangelical, he's learned things and talked with other people outside your relationship with him. So, nothing is a given.

Navigating the signals you're receiving from your confused recruit won't be easy. But don't discount your instincts. TRUST YOUR GUT. Your natural instincts are usually right, not always, but usually.

Yes, you'll likely have one shot at this. If he refuses your gesture of love, you will not have another chance. But you can't let fear hold you back. Worthwhile success is only achieved by risk. And up to now, everything you've done has been to make that risk acceptable on a cost-benefit ratio. Sorry, hope that alluding to an accounting principle didn't make you go limp.

So, if all the signals are go, including your gut …. then, during a pause in conversation, lean over and if you believe he is expecting you to act, kiss him on the lips. If he doesn't pull back, touch his crotch tenderly. If he still doesn't pull back, put your arms around him and slip him some tongue. He's yours!

Now, you're both men. And both of your have been programmed with a fair amount of sexual aggression. But this moment is a very delicate time. And showing too much aggression might be a deal-killer for him and too little also a deal killer. You need to be sensitive to what his actions and words are telling you. Though, if he hasn't say "stop faggot" I doubt there will be any words exchanged at all. Just excretions!

Perhaps, you will start tenderly massaging his penis through his pants and move on to mutual masturbation. Then some oral foreplay. And finally, anal penetration. But, it's unlikely you'll get to more than third base on the first try. Think about his feelings. He's being asked to process a lot. You might not want to go for anal penetration today.

Anal sex can be suggested by merely rubbing your penis against his ass. If he seems overwhelmed by the idea of you inside him, let him penetrate you first. Remember, your primary goal besides making him your boyfriend is to not scare him off with a sex scene heavier than he can handle. Eventually, if he is the right one, he'll reciprocate and your love affair (and tutoring) will have been launched.

And you will have begun to help make the world a better place for everyone!

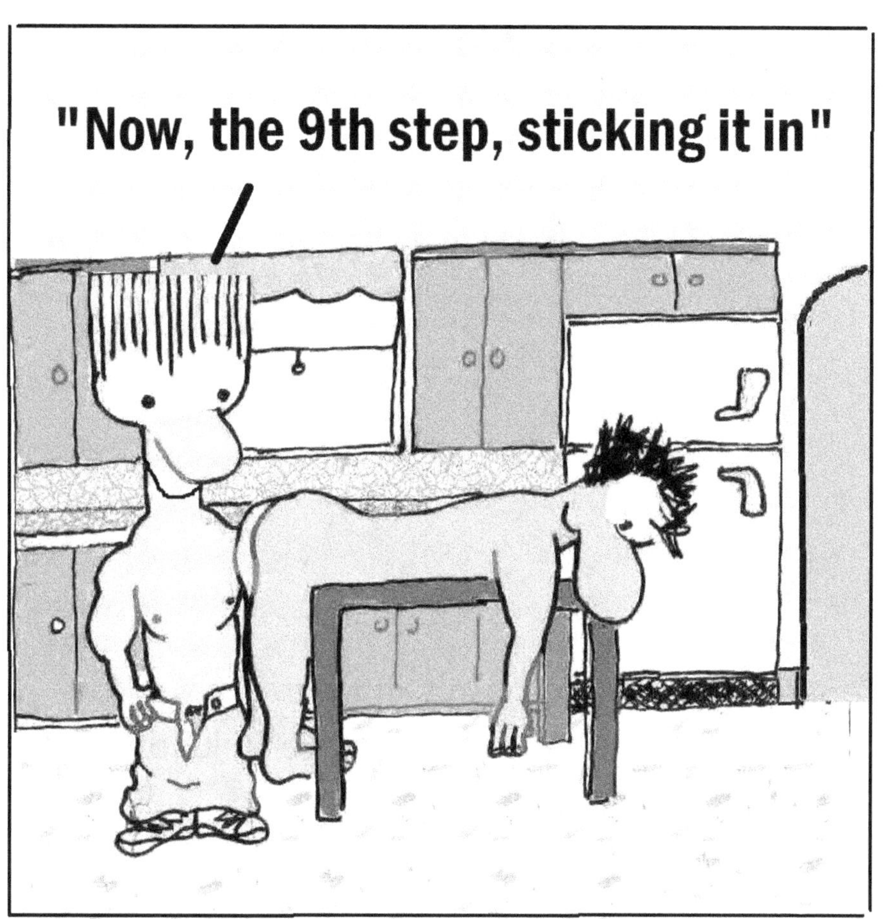

"Now, the 9th step, sticking it in"

Life With & Without Him

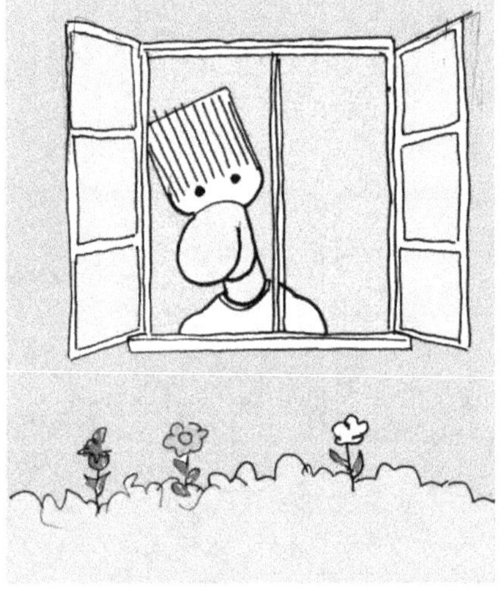

Congratulations. He hasn't murdered you. You have a new boyfriend. And you've helped him find who he really is.

But new to Gay love as he is, in most situations he's going to want to explore before he settles down with one man.

That "one man" will likely not be you, but very importantly, you will ALWAYS be his friend and mentor. In the coming months and years, it will be up to you to provide him the intellectual resources and emotional support for his new, non-evangelical life style.

Remember you are on a mission **for** God, whoever God is (though we're quite sure God doesn't mind anal sex; He invented it).

Your young Evangelical's education must continue throughout your association. Make sure you keep current on all the literature that refutes the hateful Evangelical view of the world. You can "google" can't you.

Good luck. And now, who's next?

$\mathfrak{Epilogue}$

Your mission, our mission, is *on behalf* of the "God" we KNOW …. the God who created Gay men and women and wants them to live in peace and be happy.

If we are a tribe, it is a tribe of inclusion and love, not a tribe of hate and exclusion.

This book is satire that is intended to motivate thinking people everywhere to counteract the Evangelical God's lying, greedy surrogates who pretend to "know" God and wreck people's lives with their fake take on God's will.

Even if your "religion" is science, humanism, atheism – *and especially if it's Christianity* - you need to come along on this crusade. Because none of you, in any of the groups I've listed, want fake gods of any kind to rule over your lives.

But a fake god is what young Evangelical Christian men of America have been subjugated to. Everywhere, fake prophets preaching fake dogma enslave these youths into a belief in a system that is designed to incite fear and hatred for the benefit of the fake prophets themselves.

The teachings of evangelical Christianity bear virtually no resemblance to Jesus' pronouncements, nor His humanity, or decency.

Instead, greedy Evangelicals, tribalists and power-hungry politicians have hijacked Jesus' message and poisoned it with ancient superstitions from the time when night was pitch black and humans believed that disobeying dietary rules brought the wrath of the gods upon them.

Our mission for God is to demonstrate to the brain-washed Evangelical youth of America that the pathway to love begins with embracing love in all its forms.

I was raised in the Orthodox Christian Church. I was an altar boy. I loved the liturgy, all two and one-half hours of it, the theatre of it all. When my beloved grandmother died when I was 16 years old, I believed she had gone to a real place: Heaven.

But I began to take a more skeptical look at theology though when the alcoholic mortician that we hired to bury my grandmother slammed his hand hard against her casket (with a booming noise that violated the holiness of the occasion) on its way out of the church to show a pallbearer where to position himself to grab the box.

I wondered: WHAT DOES HE THINK IS INSIDE THAT BOX? The mortician doesn't seem to think it's my grandmother!

Ever since that horrifying epiphany, I've been asking what happens when we die. And, of course, the larger question, "is there a God?"

In search of answers, I read everything I could. I looked around at the world and I decided I couldn't make up my mind about God. But I was pretty sure that the God that created a dog-eat-dog world wasn't explained fully by any religion. Did Christian leaders really want me to believe that God let six million Jews go to the gas chambers just to protect Adolph Hitler's free will?

My next epiphany was the last nail in religion's coffin. I had been attracted to male bodies since I could remember seeing a naked man and being pleased by what I saw. I was only 6 years old. Years later, when I finally understood that I was homosexual, and that my sexual orientation had been selected for me, not by me, I knew that the religions that hated gays (all of them) were not at all God inspired. If priests and pastors and reverends were in touch with God, he would tell them that sexual orientation is not a choice. It is God given.

Fake Christians, Evangelical Christians, poison the well for all of us. They make Gays into monsters. It made young Christian men afraid to seek the love of other men. Indeed, this hatred of Gays had spread even outside the church into the general population of less-than-religious men.

As a youth, many relationships with men to whom I was attracted — and who liked me - were stifled by the insidious message of the fake Christians. These young men had become fake Christians themselves though they were more concerned with society's judgment than God's wrath.

It's time to put an end to this rape of the American males' mind. It's time to liberate the minds and bodies of young Christian men everywhere! Starting with the Evangelicals.

It's time to rewrite religious history and the rules of masculinity. One Evangelical young man at a time. Onward and upward … up their sweet asses!

Congratulations!

You've reached THE END of the beginning.
Get out there and pound some evangelical ass!

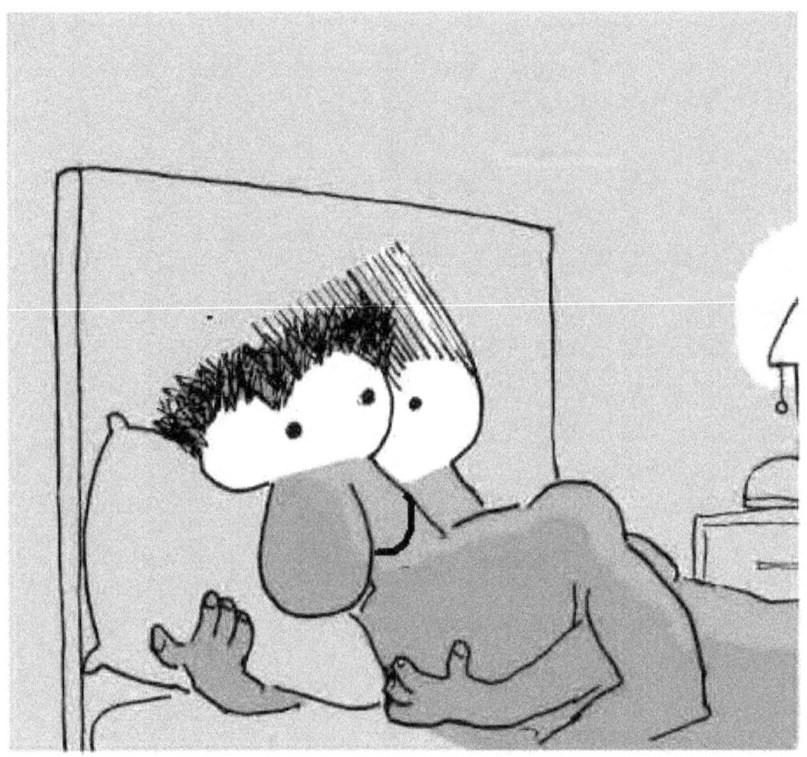

"HOW TO POUND SOME SENSE
INTO A RELIGIOUS NUT JOB"
A PYGA MEDIA BOOK
In collaboration with Amazon.com
©2018 BY JAKichi